Storytime Stickers

Day of the Dragons

By Carol Murray

Illustrated by Lisa Perrett

STERLING and the distinctive Sterling logo are
registered trademarks of Sterling Publishing Co., Inc.

2 4 6 8 10 9 7 5 3 1

Published by Sterling Publishing Co., Inc.
387 Park Avenue South, New York, NY 10016
Text © 2008 by Carol Murray
Illustrations © 2008 by Lisa Perrett
Distributed in Canada by Sterling Publishing
C/o Canadian Manda Group, 165 Dufferin Street
Toronto, Ontario, Canada M6K 3H6
Distributed in the United Kingdom by GMC Distribution Services
Castle Place, 166 High Street, Lewes, East Sussex, England BN7 1XU
Distributed in Australia by Capricorn Link (Australia) Pty. Ltd.
P.O. Box 704, Windsor, NSW 2756, Australia

Sterling ISBN-13: 978-1-4027-4659-8
ISBN-10: 1-4027-4659-8

For information about custom editions, special sales, premium and
corporate purchases, please contact Sterling Special Sales
Department at 800-805-5489 or specialsales@sterlingpublishing.com.

STERLING

New York / London
www.sterlingpublishing.com/kids

In eye-popping spirals and dives,
a gaggle of dragons arrives.
With backpacks and cell phones, and flip-flops as well,
they've taken some rooms at the *Ritzy Hotel.*

Now they've gone for a swim in the pool.
No Running! for that is the rule.
They slip to the bathhouse in singles or doubles,
and swim underwater and blow steamy bubbles.

Soon they're off for a long mountain hike,
and someone is riding a bike.
Their backpacks are brimming with apples and dips,
and water to moisten their fire-breathing lips.

Then it's back to the gym for a while,
where they jog on the treadmills with style.
The balance beam beckons. They walk it with ease,
and flip to the floor mat and sink to their knees.

The fountain's a fine place to shower,
so that's where they spend the next hour.
With bright yellow duckies and boats on the scene,
they splash in the water and scrub themselves clean.

Then they fluff and get dressed in fine clothes.

Taking pictures, they giggle and pose.

And they skip to a room where a banquet is spread,

cucumber salad, lasagne, and bread.

And soon they are ready to dance,
in a tail-dragging wiggle and prance.
The ballroom has lanterns that flicker and glow,
and star-studded streamers that add to the show.

Then it's back to their rooms for the night,
where they join in a grand pillow fight,
and a marshmallow roast with petite puffs of fire.
Then they crawl into bed, for it's time to retire.